PATRICK
APOSTLE
OF
ULSTER;

A
Protestant
View
Of
Patrick

Nelson McCausland

**Published by the Grand Orange Lodge of Ireland
Education Committee**

GOLI Publications
The Grand Orange Lodge of Ireland
65 Dublin Road, Belfast. BT2 7HE
Northern Ireland
E-Mail: goli@orange.thegap.com

British Library Cataloguing -in -Publication Data
A Catalogue record for this book is
available from the British Library

McCausland, Nelson
 Patrick : Apostle of Ulster : a Protestant view of Patrick
 1. Patrick, Saint 2. Christian saints - Ireland - Biography
 3. Ireland - Church history - To 1172
 I. Title
 270'.092

ISBN 0 9501444 5 2

CONTENTS

FOREWARD

Ireland is a land well known for its myths and legends, this is particularly true when it comes to its 'Patron Saint', Patrick.

The Emerald Isle is not unique in this respect. The other 'Patron Saints', David of Wales, George of England and Andrew of Scotland fall into a similar category as the mists of time surround them with their own particular myths and legends. Indeed it could be argued that there is more evidence for the place and work of Patrick than for any of them.

Because of the popular pictures and statues of Patrick, with his bishop's mitre and staff, it is sometimes unwittingly assumed by many that Patrick was part of 'Roman' Ireland with his allegiance to the 'Roman See'. Nothing could be further from the truth and there is little evidence to substantiate such a claim.

It is the function of the Education Committee of the Grand Orange Lodge of Ireland '. . . . *to educate the Brethren of our Institution and the general public in the truths and principles of the Reformed Religion, and our historical and cultural heritage.'* Accordingly we present this Protestant View Of Patrick' by a member of the Education Committee, Nelson McCausland, to whom we are indebted for such excellent research and comprehensive writing.

As we present this publication to the general public we are conscious of the desire on the part of many in these days to 'listen to the other side'. It is our prayer that this publication may contribute to a better understanding of the Culture and Traditions of the majority population of the northern part of this island.

Brian Kennaway
Convenor
GOLI Education Committee
March 1997

PATRICK
APOSTLE OF ULSTER;
A
Protestant
View
Of
Patrick

"The last missionary enterprise of the British church before it sank under the impact of the Anglo-Saxon invasion was the firm establishment of the Christian faith in Ireland. The leader and moving spirit of this undertaking was the bishop Patricius, or Patrick, who thus may also be credited with having made possible the Christianising by the Irish of their Pictish and Anglo-Saxon neighbours."

T O'Raifeartaigh
[Encyclopaedia Britannica 13:1077]

INTRODUCTION

Saint Patrick wasn't Irish. He wasn't sent to Ireland by the Pope. He didn't wear a bishop's mitre and he didn't drive the snakes out of Ireland.

Much that is popularly believed about Saint Patrick is simply fiction and fantasy. But what are the real facts about Patrick? What do we really know about him?

Patrick was the son of a British churchman. He was captured by raiders and spent six years as a slave in Ulster. There he was converted and later he escaped back to his home and family. Some years after this he heard the call of God to come across to the island of Ireland and preach the gospel.

His ministry covered the length and breadth of Ulster and through his preaching many became Christians. Churches were built and men of God were ordained to minister in those churches. Patrick was God's man for Ulster, the Apostle of Ulster.

SOURCES

The Writings of Patrick

Patrick is known primarily from his two short works, the *Confession* and the *Epistle*, which were described by Sir Samuel Ferguson as 'the oldest documents in British history'.

According to T O'Raifeartaigh:
> "The authenticity of these sources is unquestioned."
> [Encyclopaedia Britannica 13:1077]

In these works Patrick bares his soul to us. As the Patrician scholar D A Binchy points out:
> "The moral and spiritual greatness of the man shines through every stumbling sentence of his *rustic* Latin."

(a) Epistle

This is a letter of protest against an outrage carried out by the soldiers of a British prince called Coroticus. This is the Latinised form of a name which is elsewhere given as Caradoc. His soldiers had carried off a number of newly converted Christians and had sold them as slaves. Patrick had already sent a letter by messenger to Coroticus asking him to return those whom he had abducted but he and his soldiers had laughed at the request. Now Patrick protests against their crime and denounces what they have done. He also excommunicates Coroticus and demands the return of the captives.

(b) Confession

The *Confession* is a spiritual autobiography, which Patrick wrote in his old age. The document gets its name from a sentence in its final chapter, 'This is my confession before I die' It seems that there had been some criticism of his mission and the *Confession* is a defence of that mission, addressed to some British churchmen. Patrick affirms that he was chosen by God to do his work, although he was unworthy and uneducated. He also expresses his praise and gratitude to God who called him to this work.

The *Confession* is a longer and later work than the *Epistle*. Nevertheless it is quite short, only sixty two paragraphs long and with numerous gaps. As Liam de Paor comments:
> "It is a disconnected narrative, breaking off in a bewildering way in the middle of a story to recount some other experience which has come to mind; ... but above all concerned with internal rather than external experience."
>
> [Milestones in Irish History p 28]

As a result it is impossible to reconstruct a detailed life of Patrick from the *Confession*.

There are about a dozen extant copies of the *Confession*, the earliest of which is contained in the *Book of Armagh*. This was copied by Ferdomnach, the scribe of Armagh, who died c 845. The other manuscripts were preserved in English and continental libraries and date from the 10th to the 12th centuries.

Both these documents are notable for their simple style and their modest claims. They are entirely free of the so-called 'miracles' which are found in the medieval Roman biographies of Patrick.

Tirechan's Memoir

Several hundred years after the death of Patrick the first of many biographies of Patrick appeared. In these biographies miracles were manufactured and multiplied to enhance the life of Patrick.

Tirechan (pronounced Teera-hawn) was a disciple of Ultan, bishop of Ardbraccan, County Meath, who furnished him with both written and oral tradition about Patrick. He refers to Ultan as no longer living, so his memoir must have been compiled after Ultan's death in 657 AD.

Tirechan was not so much writing a life of Patrick as compiling a record of Patrick's travels through Meath and Connaught. He pays little attention to the early part of Patrick's life. Indeed, with the exception of a slight introduction, the *Memoir* is confined to the work supposedly carried out by Patrick in Meath, where Ultan lived, and Connaught, which was the home country of Tirechan.

Muirchu's Biography

Muirchu (pronounced Murra-hoo) produced a more-or-less chronological narrative but he describes some of the difficulties he encountered in writing it - the doubtful sources, the divergent opinions and his own frail memory.

The date of this biography is fixed from the statement that the author wrote under the direction of Bishop Aedh from Sletty, County Laois, in the midlands. We know that Aedh died in 700 AD and so the biography must have been started before that date but it may have been completed after the death of Aedh. However, the most likely date for this work is in the second half of the 7th century.

As Rt. Rev.W S Kerr, Bishop of Down and Dromore commented in *The Independence of the Celtic Church in Ireland*:
> "It may be said that, though Muirchu and Tirechan are far more reliable than the extraordinary compilers and composers of fables who in later years wrote Lives of St Patrick, still they

indulge in all sorts of incredible stories too."
[The Independence of the Celtic Church in Ireland p 32]

Both Tirechan and Muirchu embroidered and embellished the life of Patrick with incredible wonders and miracles. They included many spurious stories and they are far from reliable but those who wrote later biographies of Patrick went even further in manufacturing and multiplying such inventions.

The Hymn of Fiacc

This is a short metrical account of Patrick and is traditionally ascribed to Fiacc, a disciple of Patrick and Bishop of Sletty, but it was actually composed much later. It refers to the desolation of Tara and could not, therefore, have been written before the middle of the 6th century. Dr Whitley Stokes ascribes it to the 8th century and Dr J H Todd to the 9th century.

Tripartite Life

The *Tripartite Life* is divided into three separate and lengthy homilies and was designed to be read as a sermon or to provide material for sermons to be preached during the three-day celebration in honour of Saint Patrick.

It was probably compiled about the end of the 9th century and in it we can see how the legend of Patrick had developed since the 7th century. The compiler based his work chiefly on Muirchu, Tirechan and other documents transcribed and indexed in the *Book of Armagh* and then added more folklore and fiction. A new set of miracles, commonly known as the childhood miracles, first appear in the *Tripartite Life*. They begin at Patrick's birth and it is claimed that the flagstone on which he was born pours forth water if anyone commits perjury on it! James F Kenney comments:

> "The Tripartite Life shows the evolution of the Patrick Legend nearly completed. Only minor elaborations have since taken place."

[The Sources for Early Irish History p 344]

The writer presents Patrick as a harsh, ill-tempered miracle-worker. It shows him sulking on the mountain top 'in evil mind' and browbeating the angel to wring greater benefits from God. We see Patrick driving his chariot three times over his sister Lupait for her unchastity. We also read of angels serving Patrick, even performing menial jobs like cleaning the hearth for him! All this is very different from the humble evangelist we find in Patrick's own writings. In effect the medieval writers invented a new 'Patrick'.

The *Tripartite Life*, in an abridged form, remained the most popular account of Patrick in Ireland until this century and it influenced later accounts of Patrick. As Kathleen Hughes states:

> "It is probably the Tripartite Life of Patrick which determines the character of many of the later Lives."
>
> [Early Christian Ireland: Introduction to the Sources p 239]

The Book of Armagh

The *Book of Armagh* was written during the early part of the 9th century by Ferdomnach, the official scribe of Armagh. It is not primarily an historical document, but would appear to have been written to enhance Armagh's claims to the primacy of the Episcopal Sees in Ireland. The manuscript is preserved in the library of Trinity College, Dublin.

Jocelin

Jocelin was a Cistercian monk from the monastery of Furness in Lancashire and he was asked by John de Courcy to write a life of Patrick. This work was commissioned to enhance the prestige of Down, just as the *Tripartite Life* had been written to increase the prestige of Armagh.

Jocelin's life of Patrick is essentially a compilation of all available material, set out in a logical manner.

Colgan's Collection

Dr John Colgan, a Franciscan, made a collection of seven *Lives*, which he published in 1647 in his *Trias Thaumaturga* (Wonder-working Triad). The triad were Patrick, Brigid and Columba. The seven were (1) Fiacc's hymn (2) an anonymous *Life* which probably belongs to the 9th or 10th century (3) an anonymous *Life* largely based on Probus (4) an anonymous Life from the 9th or 10th century (5) a *Life* by Probus,

11

written in the 10th or 11th century (6)Jocelin's *Life* of Patrick (7) the *Tripartite Life*.

Hagiography and propaganda

The writings of the lives of the saints, Idealises them.

Hagiography, the writings of the saint's lives, is often a blend of historical fact with myths and legends. Many of the later works, from the 7th century onwards, were written either to promote a person or a place or to promote a person and a place.

In the 7th century there were contacts between Ireland and Rome and there was a party in the church in Ireland who were known at the time as the *Romani* or Romanisers. It was this Romanising party which invented a mythical Patrick, linked him with Rome and then sought thereby to establish the primacy of Armagh over the churches in Ireland.

In his book *The Irish Catholic Experience*, Patrick Corish writes:
> "The effective rise of the church of Armagh, and with it the acceptance of Patrick as the national apostle, may well have drawn some of its strength from an association with the Romani: Armagh appears to have been the first northern church to join the Romanising party. Armagh's claims are set out in the *Liber Angeli*, which existed there before the end of the seventh century. These claims are extensive. Armagh claims direct authority over the north-east. It also claims, as the heir of Patrick, that every church not absorbed into the monastic *paruchiae*, is subject to Armagh, and claims further that even the monastic *paruchiae* originated in a usurpation of the universal authority of Patrick. Finally, it is claimed that Armagh is the court of appeal from all the churches in Ireland, and that appeal may be carried further, to Rome, only when the sages of Armagh are baffled".
> [The Irish Catholic Experience p 8]

In Ulster the Romanisers did not gain the ascendancy until much later but they were producing propaganda from the 7th century.

Romanisers :1)to think and act in a romantic way. 2) to interpret according to romantic precepts. 3) to make or become romantic in style.

Hagiography and history

Up until the latter part of the last century most writers simply accepted the medieval accounts of Patrick and repeated them. They made little attempt to cut away the legendary embellishment and extricate Patrick from the legends and myths surrounding him.

The first serious attempt in modern times to approach the story of Patrick in a scholarly manner was made by Rev Professor J H Todd, a Church of Ireland clergyman, who published a life of Patrick in 1864. Since then much good work has been done is rediscovering the historical Patrick.

As Bishop R P C Hanson has pointed out:
> "All the exciting and glamorous features that tradition has attached to Patrick must be removed if we wish to know what he was really like. And yet the historical Saint Patrick is more interesting and more worth studying than all these later gaudy traditions."
>
> [The Life and Writings of the Historical Saint Patrick p 1,2]

Unfortunately many Roman Catholic writers and others persist in propagating the legends and myths which were invented by medieval writers and many publishers persist in publishing such books. There is obviously a market for such material and some people prefer the mythical Patrick to the historical Patrick.

Patrick was born in Britain towards the end of the 4th century. But what was Britain like at that time?

A Roman army invaded Britain in 43 AD and within a few years they had conquered the lower part of the country. The mountain tribes of Wales and the north held out longer while the Scots were never finally conquered. Hadrian's Wall still marks the frontier which long ago the Roman legions held against the Scots. Further north there was another wall which was built in 142 AD by order of the emperor Antoninus and was known as the Antonine Wall. This ran across Scotland between the River Clyde and the Firth of forth. The Romans allowed the Picts to occupy the land between the two walls but the district was reclaimed by Valentian in 368 AD and renamed 'Valentia' after him.

Britain was a Roman province, ruled by Roman governors, visited by Roman emperors, colonised by Roman citizens and kept in order by Roman legions. It became almost as civilised and cultured as any other part of the Roman Empire and this continued for 300 years.

A network of roads was developed, stately houses and villas were constructed and garrison towns were built in important centres. The Romans brought with them their religion with its pantheon of pagan gods.   *collection of gods*

However the time came when the Roman soldiers were needed back on the continent to defend Italy against invasion and Britain was gradually evacuated.

THE ANCIENT BRITISH CHURCH

The Christian faith was introduced to Britain at an early date, probably in the first century, and was firmly established by the time of Patrick.

Tertullian at the end of the second century and Origen about forty-five years later both state that by their time the Christian faith had penetrated Britain. In his book *Adversus Judaeos* (c 7) he said:

> 'Britannorum inaccessa Romanis loca Christo vero subdita.'
> "Those parts of the British Isles which were yet unapproached by the Romans were yet subject to Christ."

14

In 314 three British bishops attended the Council of Arles. They were Eborius of York, Restitutus of London and Adelphius, probably of Lincoln. This suggests that by that time Christianity had spread over a large area of Britain. Another church council was held at Rimini in 359 and again a number of British bishops attended. Indeed throughout the 4th century we can trace the steady expansion of Christianity.

PATRICK

Patrick's original name is said to have been Succat, Patricius being his Latin name.

It is not possible to say with any certainty when Patrick was born but John R Walsh and Thomas Bradley state:
> "The conservative dating of about 432-461 for Patrick's mission and a birth-date c 385, is now ... generally accepted.
> [A History of the Irish Church p 16]

In his letter to Coroticus, Patrick refers to the Franks as still heathen. This indicates that the letter was written between 451, the date generally accepted as that of the Franks' entry into Gaul as far as the Somme River, and 496, when they were baptised en masse. This places the letter and therefore part of his ministry within the second half of the 5th century.

PATRICK'S FAMILY

Patrick was born into a Christian home and his family had been a Christian family for at least two generations. His grandfather was called Poitus. His father Calpurnius was a deacon and a minor local official. There was nothing unusual in this because celibacy was not enforced in the early church.

These names Patrick (Patricius), Calpurnius and Poitus are all Roman names and so Patrick was a free-born citizen of the Roman empire.

In the *Confession* as we now have it, Patrick himself makes no mention of his mother. But the author of the fourth Life in Colgan's collection quotes the *Confession* as stating that his mother's name was Concessa. It is possible that an earlier version of the *Confession* than any still in existence may have contained this information. But an ancient writing *On the Mothers of the Saints of Ireland*, attributed to Aengus the Culdee in the 9th century, says that his mother was Ondbahum of the Britons. In the *Tripartite Life* the story of Concessa was further elaborated and she is said to have been a relative, possibly a sister, of Martin of Tours, thereby linking Patrick with the most prestigious figure of continental monasticism. Jocelin also claims that she was a sister of Martin but such claims are rather late and therefore doubtful.

PATRICK'S BIRTHPLACE

Patrick says that his father owned a farm or villa near the village of Bannaven Taberniae. This is the only clue to Patrick's birthplace but scholars disagree about its location. Muirchu says that it was 'not far distant from our sea' and it certainly makes sense to think of a location close to the west coast of Britain. The Irish raiders would have concentrated their attacks on the western shore of Britain. It is unlikely that they would have raided the east coast and unlikely that they would have penetrated far inland.

In Scotland there is a local legend that Patrick was born at Old Kilpatrick, near Dumbarton. Dumbarton, with its great basalt rock rising up from the banks of the Clyde, was the western terminal point of the Antonine Wall which Antoninus Pius, the adopted son and successor of Hadrian, erected across Scotland about the year 144 AD. At one time this tradition was rejected because there was no archaeological evidence for the existence of Roman villas in south-west Scotland but in recent years evidence has emerged of Roman villas in the Strathclyde region and much academic opinion now favours this as the region where Patrick was born.

However, others look further south and suggest that Patrick was born in Cumbria or even in Wales. The Latin name has been altered by some scholars to read ' Banna Venta Bernia' and his birthplace located at Birdoswald, near Carlisile, in Cumbria.

The fact that Patrick's family owned a villa and had servants suggests that he had a comfortable life and was well provided for during his early years.

16

5th CENTURY IRELAND

In the 5th century Ireland was divided into a large number of small tribal areas or *tuatha*. The *tuath*, which means 'a people', was the basic political entity and each of them was quite independent under its elected king. There were about one hundred and fifty of these *tuatha* in Ireland. However, from about the beginning of the Christian era, there had been a process of political cohesion and eventually the island was divided into five groups of *tuatha*, known as the *'five fifths of Ireland'*- Munster, Connaught, Leinster, Meath and Ulster. But at the time of Patrick Ulster itself was divided and there were three independent kings in Ulster.

As regards the history of Ireland in the 5th century very little is known. Professor Gearoid MacNiocaill commented that, "The fifth century has been very justly described as a lost century." This view is supported by Professor Charles Thomas who said that, "The fifth century continues to be the most obscure in our recorded history."

[The Living Legend of St Patrick p 12]

In the time of Patrick Ireland had a very small population, around a quarter of a million people. The population of Ulster would therefore have been around fifty thousand. This was a totally rural and agrarian society. In fact there were no towns in Ireland until the arrival of the Vikings. The people lived in ring-forts, crannogs and unenclosed houses.

It is thought that there were as many as forty thousand ring-forts in the island and the most common form of ring fort was the rath. This was a circular open space surrounded by a bank and a palisade. The ring fort enclosed houses and farm buildings and provided some form of protection. The houses were made of wood plastered over with clay and roofed with thatch.

Crannogs are man-made islands in lakes and bogs and they are much less numerous than ring forts. The poorest people lived in unenclosed houses.

Much of the land was covered with thick forests and with bogs. It was the extent of its forests which in early times gained for Ireland the name of *Innis-na-Beeva* or Island of the Woods. Wild animals roamed freely through the countryside. There were great herds of deer, wild boars with long tusks and even wolves.

The people were a farming people and, as well as the forests and bogs, there were large open plains where they grew crops and grazed their cattle, pigs and sheep. However they supplemented their farming by hunting.

It was a century of turmoil across Europe, as barbarian hordes destroyed the Roman empire and sacked the city of Rome, and the Angles and Saxons invaded Great Britain. This was the start of the Dark Ages but in contrast to this Ireland was comparatively peaceful.

For Ireland the 5th century marked the end of centuries of isolation and the start of the island's entry into the historical world.

DRUIDISM

Professor James Heron comments:
> "The religion of the ancient Irish was Druidical but the popular idea of that religion is quite erroneous. It included belief in the immortality of the soul and in the doctrine of a day of judgement - doctrines doubtless which, along with others, made them more ready to accept of Christianity."
>
> [The Celtic Church in Ireland p 41]

The religion of the people was Druidism but what exactly was this religion? Among the ancient Celts, the Druids were a class of priests and learned men. They formed an important part of every Celtic community in Ireland, Britain, and Gaul, and their leaders often rivalled kings and chiefs in prestige, if not power. They seem to have served as judges as well as priests, and their counsel was eagerly sought by all classes of society.

It is known that oak trees and mistletoe played an important part in Druidic rituals. It was also believed that there were special powers associated with stone, wood and water. In his *History of the Church of Ireland,* Bishop Richard Mant describes the ritual which survived to his day and which was associated with a well in county Monaghan. At this place of pilgrimage there was a stone which was reputed to bear the mark of the knee of Saint Patrick, a cross he was supposed to have

18

erected and an alder tree which was said to have sprung up where the saint blessed the ground. The ritual associated with this well involved the pilgrims kissing the stone and placing their knee in the indentation, saying various prayers and bowing to the cross, the stone and the alder tree. When the rite was completed the water taken from the adjacent well would cure sick cattle! Such customs and rituals have survived since pre-Christian times and show us something of the nature of the pre-Christian religion of the island.

It is remarkable that worship which was opposed by Patrick is now associated with him!

SLAVERY

From about the middle of the 3rd century Latin writings makes frequent reference to raids which were carried out by the Irish, who were known as the Scotti. Irish traditions also suggest that such attacks took place. In the second half of the 4th century, when Roman power in Britain was beginning to break down, the raids became more frequent. These Irish raiders sailed in curraghs, wooden framed boats covered in hides, which were fast and seaworthy, capable of negotiating the stormy waters of the Irish Sea. As E Estyn Evans said:

"The sea-going curraghs were ideal craft for the Irish raiders who plundered west Britain during and after the Roman occupation: light in weight, of shallow draught and capable of flying over the waves."

[Irish Folk Ways p 237]

Around 400 AD, when he was 16 years of age, a band of Irish pirates raided the countryside where Patrick lived. They hunted down the terrified people and robbed them of their possessions. Some of the people were slaughtered and years later Patrick recalled that:

"They murdered the servants, men and women, of my father's household."

Others like Patrick were taken away by the raiders in their ships to be sold as slaves in Ireland. Again Patrick recalled:

"With many thousands of others I was carried off into captivity in Ireland."

SLEMISH

Patrick was sold as a slave to a man named Milchu who was a Cruithin chief and who lived at Skerry in County Antrim. About five miles away from Skerry across the River Braid stands the hill of Slemish (*Sliabh Mis*, *Mis* being a woman's name). There on the slopes around Slemish Patrick spent six bleak years as a herdsman of sheep and pigs.

Patrick does not mention the place of his captivity but Slemish in County Antrim is the traditional location of the captivity.
Some recent writers have sought to locate it at Killala in County Mayo. However there are a number of objections to this. Firstly, if this sacred spot had been in Connaught, Tirechan, as a Connaught man, would certainly have set out the claim of Connaught but he did not and in fact he accepted the claim of Slemish. Secondly, one of the obvious objections to Killala is that it is in a relatively flat region whereas Slemish is consistent with Patrick's reference to a mountainous region.

[Confession 16]

Professor Donal Kerr writes:
> "Tradition tells us that it was in County Antrim, on Slemish mountain, that Patrick spent six years of harsh slavery. He himself does not name the place but speaks of the snow and frost and rain in mountain and forest; certainly Slemish with its view of the heartland of Ulster was bleak, cold and forbidding."

[Saint Patrick p 5]

Between Slemish and Skerry there is a townland called Ballyligpatrick (the townland of Patrick's hollow). In it are the remains of an ancient rath.

Patrick was in a strange land, perhaps often cold and hungry, surrounded by a people speaking a language he did not know. But during the years of his captivity Patrick acquired a good knowledge of the local language and also made himself acquainted with the religion, habits and customs of the people. Although he did not know it at the time, all this would be of great advantage to him during his future mission.

CONVERSION

But the most important thing that Patrick gained in Ulster during his captivity was personal salvation.

There on the Antrim hillside, far away from his family, his friends and the comforts of home, Patrick had ample time for reflection. Although he had been brought up in a Christian family, Patrick says that at the time of his captivity he did not know the true God. But the Spirit of God began to work in his heart and his thoughts turned to the God of his fathers.

Paul Gallico expressed it well when he said:
> "During this period Patrick found God and God found Patrick and thereafter, to the end of the saint's days, neither ever abandoned the other. No man ever served God more faithfully, intensely and unswervingly than Patrick."
>
> [The Steadfast Man p 28]

ESCAPE

One night in a dream, six years after his capture, Patrick heard a voice speaking to him. The voice said that there was a ship ready and that in it he could escape .

Patrick fled from his master and made a journey of some two hundred Roman miles which would be equivalent to one hundred and eighty English miles. From Slemish this would have taken him as far as Wicklow, where there is a tradition that a point north of the town was the place of Patrick's departure. This was a difficult and dangerous journey which took him through forests and across boglands but eventually he reached the port and found the promised ship.

Patrick coaxed the captain to take him on board. At first the captain refused but later he relented and Patrick sailed away from the shores of Ireland. He reached land after three days.

Some time after his return to Britain Patrick had a dream which was similar to Paul's vision at Troas. Just as Paul, so Patrick saw a man named Victoricus gave him a letter headed 'The Voice of the Irish'. He was invited to return to the land of his captivity:

> "We beseech thee, holy youth, that thou come and walk amongst us once more."

In his account of the vision Patrick mentions the people 'who were near the Wood of Voclut which is close to the Western Sea.'

[Confession 23]

Silva Focluti or the Wood of Voclut is the only place name in Ireland which is mentioned by Patrick and its location has been the subject of much debate.

Tirechan, who compiled a life of Patrick in the late 7th or early 8th century identified it with the Wood of Fochloth in Connaught, a name which is said to survive in Faughill, near Killala, County Mayo. However Tirechan was a native of that district and this may have influenced his opinion!

J B Bury went further than Tirechan. He noted that the call to Patrick was to come and walk among them 'again' and then assumed that the call must have come from the region of Patrick's earlier slavery. From this he concluded that the six years of Patrick's captivity were spent in County Mayo and not at Slemish.

[Life of St Patrick p 27ff]

Now Patrick certainly tells us that the Wood of Voclut was 'close to the Western Sea' but that does not necessarily place it on the west coast of Ireland for in the ancient world the Irish Sea was referred to as the Western Sea.

Eoin MacNeill supposed that Voclut was a textual corruption and that the true reading was 'the Wood of Uluti', which he located near Lough Neagh.

[Proceedings of the Royal Irish Academy XXXVI (1921-24) p 249ff]

But even if the call came from the west coast of the island that does not require that Patrick's captivity be spent there. It is possible to read too much into the word 'again'.

Patrick had suffered at the hands of people from Ireland. They had taken him captive and they had kept him enslaved for six years. Yet, his heart was not filled with hatred for them. Instead he had a genuine Christian love for them and a desire to see them turn from their idols to the true God. At the close of his book on the life and work of Patrick, Canon G A Chamberlain said:

> "St Patrick had been deeply wronged by the people of this land. By their hands he had been torn from his home as a child and held in slavery. But he never paused to brood over the wrongs done him or nursed the lurking grudge. He sought no revenge save the revenge of serving those who had wronged him. In the spirit of the great Apostle, he had the grace to forget those things which are behind, and to press on to the better future. In the spirit of his Master, Christ, he set himself to love those who had despitefully treated him.."

> [St Patrick: His Life and Work p 121,122]

PREPARATION FOR HIS MISSION

Before his return to Ireland as an evangelist Patrick had to prepare himself for his mission but Patrick himself tells us nothing of that preparation. However, Muirchu and Tirechan claim that Patrick spent a considerable time on the continent and there received his education.

Muirchu's version.

According to Muirchu, Patrick spent seven years 'in his own country with his relatives' and then:

> "set out to visit and honour the apostolic see, the head, that is, of all the churches in the whole world. So he crossed the sea to the south of Britain and began to travel through Gaul. But on his way he found a very holy man of approved faith and doctrine, bishop of the city of Auxerre, leader of almost all Gaul, the great Germanus."

After studying for thirty or forty years with Germanus at Auxerre in central France, Patrick set out for Ireland but soon news reached him of the death of Germanus and he was consecrated a bishop by Amathorex. Elsewhere, however, Muirchu alludes to his consecration as a bishop by Germanus.

23

Tirechan's version.

Tirechan's account of Patrick includes the three so-called *Sayings of Patrick*.

> **1.** I had the fear of God as my guide through Gaul and Italy and the islands in the Tyrrhene Sea.
>
> **2.** You have gone from this world to paradise, thanks be to God.
>
> **3.** Church of the Irish, or rather of the Romans! in order that you may be Christians like the Romans, you must chant in your churches at every hour of prayer that commendable utterance: *Kyrie Eleison, Christe Eleison.* Let every church which follows me sing, *Kyrie Eleison, Christe Eleison.* Thanks be to God.

Elsewhere Tirechan refers to Patrick seven years travelling 'on water, is plains, and in mountain valleys throughout Gaul and the whole of Italy and this lands in the Tyrrhene Sea.' [III,1(vi)] He quotes Bishop Ultan as one of his sources that Patrick stayed for thirty years 'in one of these islands, which is called Aralanensis.' This has often been identified with the monastic island settlement on the island of Lerins off the coast of Provence.

Tirechan wanted to link Patrick with the continent and with Rome and we may safely regard these spurious sayings and claims as having been invented for that purpose.

British training.

Bishop R P C Hanson has shown clearly and authoritatively, that Patrick is 'wholly the product of the British Church', that his mission was sponsored by British churchmen and that his language is typical of the Vulgar Latin of 5th century Britain. Patrick may have visited Gaul but his Christian training was obtained from the British church.

We know nothing of the actual training that Patrick received but during that period he must have acquired that profound knowledge of the Bible which his writings reflect.

Patrick had completed his training but nevertheless, for a long time, he was reluctant to respond to the call. Even on the eve of re-embarkation for Ireland he was beset by doubts.

EARLIER CHRISTIANS IN IRELAND

The earliest reference to Christianity in Ireland comes from Tertullian, who wrote about the year 200. In his book *Adversus Judaeos* (c 7) he said:

> 'Britannorum inaccessa Romanis loca Christo vero subdita.'
> "Those parts of the British Isles which were yet unapproached by the Romans were yet subject to Christ."
>
> [Religion of the Ancient Irish Saints p 9]

Tertullian referred to the *British Isles* (plural) thereby including the island of Ireland. His claim is something of an exaggeration in that Christianity was not the dominant religion but it is clear that several hundred years before Patrick there were Christians in Ireland.

Apart from Tertullian there is considerable evidence that the south of Ireland had received the Christian message before Patrick and that there were already churches established there. This has been attributed to the work of British missionaries but may also have been due in part to the influence of Irish colonists returning home or to traders visiting Ireland. There is also the possibility that some Christians from Europe sought refuge in Ireland during the barbarian invasions of what is now France at the start of the 5th century.

Ailbhe of Emly, Ibhar of Beccere, Ciaran of Saiger, Declan of Ardmore and others laboured as missionaries in the south of Ireland before Patrick, while Auxilius, Secundinus and Iserninus are associated with the east midlands and were probably among the first Christians to organise churches there. In *A History of the Irish Church* John R Walsh and Thomas Bradley comment:

> "Most of these were probably British by birth, to judge by their names, and most are associated with the south and the south-east of the country."
>
> [A History of the Irish Church p 5]

The available evidence convinced the Celtic scholar Professor Thomas F O'Rahilly that:

> "Irish Christianity owes its origin to Britain. ... Already before 431 no small part of the population of the south-east and south of Ireland must have been converted by British missionaries."
>
> [A History of the Irish Church p 5]

Indeed down to the end of the 7th century Kildare attempted to establish the primacy for itself and even the *Book of Armagh* acknowledges that Lommanus's church at Trim was founded thirty years before Armagh itself.

Patrick states in his *Confession* that he travelled to parts 'where Christians were not'. In the past this was thought to mean that there were no Christians in the whole of Ireland before Patrick but it now seems more likely that he is simply referring to Ulster, which had not been evangelised, and that there were already Christian churches and missionaries in the midlands and the south.

PALLADIUS

In the *Chronicle of Prosper of Aquitaine*, a contemporary source, it is recorded under the year 431:

> "Palladius, ordained by Pope Celestine, is sent to the Scotti [Irish] who believe in Christ, as their first bishop".

This suggests that there were already Christians in Ireland at that time and that there were sufficient to warrant the appointment of a bishop. Palladius is also mentioned in the *Annals of Ulster* and the *Annals of Innisfallen*, but these were compiled at a much later date.

The fragments of topographical information that cling to the name of Palladius locate his mission in Leinster. However, according to tradition, Palladius' mission had little success and he was forced to leave within a few months, disappointed and discouraged. It seems that he went from Ireland to Scotland and died there soon afterwards. There are a number of churches in southern Scotland dedicated to Saint Paldy.

A THIRTY YEAR MISSION

Patrick sailed north, probably intending to visit the area where he had been a captive. Eventually he landed at the mouth of the Slaney River between Strangford and the River Quoile, on the east coast of County Down.

This was start of an evangelistic mission which was to span around thirty years and was to see the Christian message spread across Ulster.

SAUL

Patrick walked about two miles from where he landed and came to the low hill now known as Saul. There he met the local chieftain Dichu and spoke to him of Christ. Dichu was converted and gave Patrick a barn in which to hold his services. The Gaelic word for a barn is *sabhall* (now pronounced Saul) and this is the origin of the place name. This was the first church founded by Patrick and Saul has been the site of a Christian witness ever since. It is remarkable, however, that the same name, *sabhall*, was also given to a church at Armagh.

Eventually an Abbey was built at Saul. It was restored by the Bishop of Down in the 12th century but destroyed by Edward Bruce, brother of Robert Bruce of Scotland, in 1316. All that remains of the abbey today is one wall and two small cells.

A parish church was built on the site of the old abbey in 1788. This was replaced in 1932 by the present Church of Ireland building, which was erected to commemorate the 1500th anniversary of the landing of Patrick.

It is noteworthy that from the time of Patrick churches and monasteries were very numerous in all that district about Strangford Lough, where Patrick landed and laboured, and also further south round Dundrum Bay towards the Mourne Mountains.

Patrick began his mission in Saul and there, according to one tradition, he died.

ARMAGH

It seems to have been at an early period that Patrick founded a mission settlement near Armagh, a very ancient and important site.

As far back as 300 BC Macha, the warrior queen of Ulster, had established her royal residence at Emania, near Armagh, and it became the capital of the ancient kingdom of Ulster.

It is often said that the Protestant cathedral in Armagh stands on the traditional site of the church built by Patrick but according to Rev W P Carmody:

"The site of the present cathedral is not that of the first church - which was in the lower ground, known as Na Ferta."
[The Church of Ireland AD 432-1932 p 33]

Patrick established a church at Armagh but it had no position of primacy over other churches. A number of centuries after Patrick Armagh gradually established a position of prominence but it was not until the Romanisation of the church by Malachy in the 11th century that the present system of dioceses was developed and Armagh was raised to the primacy.

DOWNPATRICK

The first recognisable township was centred around the great dun or rath now known as Cathedral Hill. It was known as *Rath Celtair* and Celtair was one of the Red Branch Knights.

In the 6th century it was recorded that there was a great church at *Dun-de-leth-glas*, the ancient name of Downpatrick. At that time the town was an important religious and academic centre. A *dun* was a circular fortified enclosure

Near Downpatrick is Inch Abbey where a church has existed since the time of Patrick or soon afterwards. In 1187 the resident monks were removed by the Anglo-Norman baron John de Courcy. He built a new abbey and installed monks of the Cistercian Order, brought from Furness. There are extensive ruins of the Cistercian monastery but all that remains now of the ancient church is a sculpture preserved nearby in Inch Parish Church.

John de Courcy had arrived in Ireland in 1177 with a force of 330 men and headed north to Ulster. He captured Downpatrick and within six months he was in control of Ulster.

ULSTER

It is now generally recognised that most of Patrick's missionary work was carried out in Ulster. The historian Jonathan Bardon states:
"Most places traditionally associated with Patrick ... are in the northern half of Ireland and it was probably in Ulster that he did most of his work."
[A History of Ulster p 15]

This is also the view of Professor Hugh Kearney.

> "The likelihood is that he confined himself to the kingdom of the Ulaid with its capital at Emain Macha."

[The British Isles]

But what was the extent of Ulster during the ministry of Patrick? Kathleen Hughes answers this question:

> "When Patrick first set up his church in Ulster, that province must still have spread over much of northern Ireland, as it does in the Tain. Armagh was certainly part of Ulster. Why else should an important church be established so close to the pagan sanctuary and royal residence of the Ulster kings? The expansion of the Ui Neill began in the 5th century at Ulster's expense and the contraction of Ulster took a long time. Its final stages were probably not achieved until the first half of the seventh century."

[Early Christian Ireland: Introduction to the Sources p 230]

It was in Ulster that Patrick was converted; it was in Ulster that Patrick preached; it was in Ulster that Patrick died; and it was in Ulster soil that Patrick was buried. We are therefore entitled to describe Patrick as the Apostle of Ulster

PATRICK THE PREACHER

Patrick was a passionate and persuasive preacher. His knowledge of the Bible was remarkable and formidable. W S Kerr commented:

> "In almost every paragraph of his writings St Patrick's devotion to the Holy Scriptures is made plain. His intimate knowledge of the whole Bible is amazing. His mind is so saturated with it that his thoughts naturally, as if unconsciously, clothe themselves in Biblical phraseology."

[The Church of Ireland AD 432-1932 p 40]

If that was true of his writing it must also have been true of his preaching. His sermons must have been saturated with Scripture.

Patrick also had an impregnable sense of a divine commission. 'I make no false claim,' he wrote to Coroticus, 'I have part with those whom He called and predestinated to preach the gospel.' Yet he was a most humble-minded man. He began his Confession by saying:

"I am Patrick, a sinner, most unlearned, the least of all the faithful, and utterly despised by many."

Moreover he offered praise constantly to God for having chosen him to be the instrument whereby many who had worshipped 'idols and unclean things' had become 'the people of God'.

Patrick combined strength and selflessness and he suffered much for the Lord he served during his ministry. Towards the end of the *Confession* he wrote:

"I expect daily to be killed, betrayed, or brought back into slavery, or something of the kind."

'THE FOOTSTEPS OF PATRICK'

Right across the British Isles there are place names which include the name of Patrick. In Scotland there are places such as Kilpatrick (church of Patrick), Dalpatrick (district of Patrick), Kirkpatrick (church of Patrick) and Portpatrick; in England there is a Kirkpatrick and a Patterdale (Patrick's dale); in Wales there is a Sarn-badrig (Patrick's causeway) and a Llan-badrig (church of Patrick); on the Isle of Man there is a Kirkpatrick; and in Ireland there are so many place names which include the name of Patrick. As well as place names there are also churches, rocks, wells and many other things with which the name of Patrick is associated.

It is sometimes thought that from these place names and associations it is possible to reconstruct his movements. As one writer put it many years ago in *The Book of Days* 'the footsteps of Patrick can be traced, almost from his cradle to his grave, by the names of places called after him.' However, this is simply not so.

It was often the case that centuries after Patrick his name was attached to a church or a place with which he had no connection, either out of devotion to Patrick or to give added status to the site.

There are many wells in Ireland associated with the name of Patrick but these should not be taken to prove that Patrick actually visited those sites. Well-worship was a part of the pre-Christian religion of Ireland and over 3,000 'holy wells' have been listed in Ireland. Eventually nearly all of these came to be associated with various

Christian saints, including Patrick. This was simply part of a process of absorbing paganism into medieval church ritual. The fact that the name of a saint is associated with a well should not be taken as proof that he visited the well.

PATRICK'S POLICY

The policy of Patrick all through his ministry was to approach in the first instance the kings and chiefs and to seek to win them over to his side. He knew that with the tribal structure of society the support of the chief was necessary for him to gain access to the people and that if the chief opposed him there would be an insuperable barrier to his evangelistic mission.

There is the well-known story of Patrick preaching to King Laoghaire, the High King of Ireland, at Tara but as Bishop R P C Hanson has written:
> "There was no High-King of Ireland in his day; the colourful story of his encounter with King Loeghaire at Tara is sheer fiction."
> [The Life and Writings of the Historical Saint Patrick p 1]

It was only much later, in the 6th century, that descendants of Niall of the Nine Hostages, ruling at Tara in northern Leinster, claimed to be overkings of three provinces and later they claimed to be high kings of all Ireland but their power rarely extended over Munster or the greater part of Leinster. It was not until the reign of Brian Boru in the 11th century that there was anything like a real high kingship over all Ireland.

CHURCH ORGANISATION

Professor J C Beckett commented on the organisation of the ancient Christian church in Ireland:
> "From the beginning, Irish Christianity developed characteristics of its own. Elsewhere, the church was being built up in lands which had once formed part of the Roman empire, where the tradition of territorial divisions was strongly established; the word 'diocese' was itself taken over from the Roman administrative system. But in Ireland territorial divisions were of secondary importance; the unit of government

was an amalgamation of kinship groups dominated by a ruling family, and church organisation followed a similar pattern; the country was not cut up into dioceses but bishops were attached to particular families. Their great number (Patrick is said to have appointed 300 of them) and the nature of their position prevented them from developing the kind of authority wielded by bishops on the continent."

[A Short History of Ireland p 12]

This is also the view of Patrick Corish who writes:
"It seems most likely that the original pattern had been that there was a bishop in every tuath or petty kingdom, and as many of the tuatha were small this in itself meant that, even at the beginning, many bishops could not have been very powerful figures."

[The Irish Catholic Experience p 7]

CHURCHES

The earliest buildings used by Christians in Ireland were small churches which generally were built of wood. According to the *Tripartite Life* the standard church built by Patrick was only 27 feet in length.

Harold G Leask, who was the Inspector of National Monuments in the Irish Republic, wrote:
"A number of literary reference of early date indicate that the church and other buildings of the first centuries of Christianity in Ireland were built mainly of wood. This building custom of the Irish - then called the Scots - was known to writers in Britain of the seventh and eighth centuries, the Venerable Bede for one, as the *more Scottorum*. Thus Bede records that when St Finan of Iona, ordained and sent by the *Scots*, became Bishop of Lindisfarne in the mid-seventh century, he built for his see, not a stone church, but one entirely of sawn wood after the Scotic (ie Irish) manner, covered with reeds."

[Irish Churches and Monastic Buildings I p 5]

The fact that the first Christian churches were built of wood is confirmed by the very frequent records in the various annals of the total burning of monastic settlements. Such frequent fires indicate that the materials used were inflammable and easily destroyed.

The early Christians built their churches of wood for a number of reasons. Firstly, wood was plentiful since the country was well wooded. Secondly, a missionary church would tend to use the materials nearest to hand and especially those generally used by the local people. It seems therefore that the churches in the time of Patrick were built on the well-known 'wattle and daub' system. Timber was used for posts and beams, pliable willow and hazel was used for weaving the walls and roof, and clay was used to cover the wickerwork both inside and outside. The roof was probably thatched with straw or reeds.

But some parts of Ireland, especially on the wind-swept western coast, were not rich in timber. Sometimes therefore, where stone was plentiful, churches were built of dry stone and the foundations of an early rectangular dry stone church, set within a circular graveyard, remain at Temple Cormac, Castleward, near Strangford.

MONASTERIES

The word monastery is derived from a Greek word meaning 'to live alone' and this reflects the original monastic ideal of the desert hermits of Egypt and Syria. Gradually, such hermits came together in small communities, though they continued to seek out remote locations. Among the first monasteries to be established in the British Isles were those in Ireland from about the 5th century.

According to E Estyn Evans:
"Irish Christianity grew up within the forms of Irish life. The Celtic church was peculiar in that the centres of its life were the great monasteries: there were no cities to form the seats of powerful bishops. Instead, the founders' kin retained the ownership of the monasteries and the Celtic tradition survived in administration ..."
[Irish Folk Ways p 7]

The monasteries certainly played a significant role in the early church in Ireland but as John Ryan comments:
"In a word, the place of monasticism in the church founded by St Patrick was important but secondary. The great apostle, like all preachers of the Gospel elsewhere, relied on bishops and clergy, not on monks as such, to carry on his work, and to bring it, in due course, to completion."
[Irish Monasticism p 96]

33

Learning in the monastic schools was, as it was for Patrick, first and foremost the Scriptures.

SOME CONVERTS OF PATRICK

We know very little about the converts of Patrick but ther names of two prominent converts are still remembered.

Donard, whose name is associated with Slieve Donard, established his principal church at Maghera, near Newcastle in County Down. This was placed within an older cashel whose stone walls still circle the shell of the old church. Outside is the stump of a round tower.

Tassach was the founder of a church at *Rath Colpa* (Raholp). This church is not far from Saul, on the road to Strangford through Raholp village. The original building may well have been of wood but it was later replaced by a small stone church. Only the walls now remain of that building but it is one of the earliest Christian buildings in Ireland.

A PEOPLE OF THE BOOK

Patrick's devotion to the Bible influenced and inspired his spiritual children for the churches and centres of learning in Ireland became schools of Bible study and attracted students from various lands. As Louis Gougaud states:

> "To speak very strictly there was held to be but one science, that of the sacred Scriptures. It was that science people came chiefly to seek from the Irish doctors."
>
> [Gaelic Pioneers of Christianity p 59]

Patrick and the churches he founded stood in the tradition of the early apostolic church as a people of the Book.

DEATH AND BURIAL OF PATRICK

The *Book of Armagh*, which was written about four hundred years after Patrick's time, states that he died on 17 March and ever since this has been accepted at the traditional date of his death.

According to the *Hymn of Fiacc*, written in the 8th century, Patrick received holy communion from Saint Tassach, bishop of Raholp, just before he died but this is a late and unreliable source.

Armagh, Downpatrick and Saul have all made the claim to be the burial place of Patrick but the strongest tradition is that linking his burial with Downpatrick.

Muirchu did not assign a specific location to Patrick's burial-place while Tireachan and the *Tripartite Life* said that, like Moses, his burial place was unknown. However, the claims of Downpatrick as the burial place of Patrick were clearly set forth by Dr William Reeves, Bishop of Down, Connor and Dromore, in a letter to the board of Down Cathedral in 1875, in which he stated that there was no doubt about Downpatrick being the burial place of Saint Patrick.

In 1901 a slab of granite, bearing a cross and the word 'Patric', was placed by the antiquarian F J Bigger on the reputed grave of Patrick beside the cathedral in Downpatrick.

TWO CHURCHES IN IRELAND

As a result of Patrick's ministry in Ulster, for a time there were two churches in Ireland; the more or less amorphous group of pre-Patrician communities in southern Ireland, sometimes referred to as the 'Old Churches', and the church established in Ulster through the mission of Patrick. The Patrician church in course of time gained strength and gradually absorbed the 'Old Churches', so that they disappeared and vanished from history.

MISSIONARY OUTREACH FROM IRELAND

The establishment of a strong Christian church in Ireland was to be of importance not only for Ireland but for the rest of the British Isles and beyond.

As Professor J C Beckett has pointed out:
> "Almost at the same time as Patrick and his successors were establishing Christianity in Ireland the Anglo-Saxon invaders were destroying it throughout a great part of Britain. The British church, which had never been strong or adventurous, made little effort to evangelise them and the work of recovering the lands lost to Christianity was first undertaken by Irish missionaries."

[A Short History of Ireland p 13]

One of the first of these missionaries was Columba who left Ulster and established a monastery on the island of Iona. During the next hundred years missionaries went out from Iona to reclaim much of Scotland and northern England for Christ.

THE GREAT COMMISSION

Before His ascension into heaven Jesus Christ gave a great commission to His disciples: *"Go ye therefore, and teach all nations, baptizing them in the name of the Father, and of the Son, and of the Holy Ghost: Teaching them to observe all things whatsoever I have commanded you: and, lo, I am with you alway, [even] unto the end of the world. Amen.."*

(Matthew 28:19,20 *AV*)

Patrick played a part in fulfilling that commission. He evangelised the lost, integrated his converts into a church organisation and defined and expounded the faith of the church.

His work of evangelism he described as 'hunting and fishing'. He hunted after people because he was concerned for their souls and wanted to bring them to Christ. He fished patiently for them, as a fisher of men.

This was God's work done in God's way and thereby Patrick secured the permanence of his work in Ulster.

THE MESSAGE

In trying to ascertain the teaching of Patrick, we must go to his own writings as the direct and supreme source of information. From that source we find that the message Patrick preached in Ulster was a biblical, evangelical and Trinitarian message. It was the same message which the Apostles had preached four centuries before. It was the message which the Reformers preached a thousand years later and it is the message which evangelical Protestants still preach today. Patrick's name must go down in history with Paul, Augustine, Luther, Cranmer, Latimer, Ridley, Knox, Wesley, Spurgeon and all true preachers of the gospel.

Dr Henry E Patton, one time Bishop of Killaloe and Clonfert, summed up the message thus:

> "You must be careful to note what St Patrick's teaching was. It was essentially Scriptural. His Creed is the same Creed which we confess today. You will find the substance of it in a beautiful hymn called St Patrick's Breastplate. You will not find any of the teaching of the Roman Church about indulgences, invocation of saints, or relics, the worship of the Blessed Virgin, or the Papal infallibility. Indeed you could not expect to find them, for such doctrines and practices were not known till hundreds of years after St Patrick's time, and they are not to be found in the Bible.
>
> > Christ be with me, Christ within me,
> > Christ behind me, Christ before me,
> > Christ beside me, Christ to win me,
> > Christ to comfort and restore me.
>
> That was the burden of St Patrick's teaching."
>
> [History of the Church of Ireland p 9]

A BIBLICAL FAITH

One of the most obvious characteristics of St Patrick's writings is the extensive use which he makes of Holy Scripture. Patrick knew the Bible well and it was for him the supreme standard of truth. Moreover he assumes that his readers are also familiar with the Bible. It is therefore clear that in Patrick's time all the faithful, both ordained ministers and ordinary members of the church read the Word of God for doctrine, for reproof, for correction and for instruction in righteousness.

In his two short works, the *Confession* and the *Epistle*, Patrick frequently uses biblical quotations to express himself. He either refers to or quotes from the Old Testament 47 times and from the New Testament at least 132 times. In the New Testament Jude, James and 2 John are the only books to which he makes no reference.

A TRINITARIAN FAITH

In his *Confession* Patrick explicitly affirms the Trinitarian nature of his message.

> "There is no other God, nor was there ever in times past, nor shall there be hereafter, except God the Father unbegotten, without beginning, ... and his Son Jesus Christ, whom we affirm verily to have always existed with the Father before the creation of the world, ... And he shed on us abundantly the Holy Ghost, the gift and earnest of immortality, who makes those who believe and obey to become children of god the Father and joint heirs with Christ, whom we confess and adore as one God in the Trinity of the Holy Name."

[section 4]

Later in the *Confession* he describes the doctrine of the Holy Trinity as his Rule of Faith.

[section 14]

A CHRIST-CENTRED FAITH

Patrick speaks repeatedly of 'Christ the Lord', 'Christ my Lord' and 'Christ my God'. His devotion to the Lord Jesus Christ as the 'one mediator between God and man' is indeed obvious and Christ is always at the centre of Patrick's message. For Patrick there is but one mediator and that is Christ.

Professor N J D White states that:

> "One of the most noticeable elements in the personal life of St Patrick, as reflected in his writings, was the intensity of his devotion to our Lord Jesus Christ.'

At the annual Patrician Pilgrimage to Saul on Sunday 10 June 1984, Dr Cahal Daly, who was then Bishop of Down and Connor, spoke of "the Roman faith that Patrick brought to Ireland" and said:

"Irish Catholic faith since Patrick has never separated Christ from Mary ... Devotion to Mary is part of the Catholic faith in which Patrick was approved by Pope Leo for his mission to Ireland."

[Irish News 11 June 1984]

But the Virgin Mary is not mentioned even once by Patrick in his writings. The veneration of Mary, which is an important part of Roman Catholic devotion, did not develop until much later. The message that Patrick preached was a message of 'Christ alone' not 'Christ and Mary'.

A MESSAGE OF SALVATION

Patrick preached about sin and salvation. He starts his *Confession* by describing himself as 'Patrick the sinner'. Although he was the son of a deacon and grandson of a presbyter, and therefore had a Christian upbringing, some years passed before he came to saving faith in Christ. Of that conversion experience he says:

"The Lord opened the understanding of my unbelief, even though late, I might call my faults to remembrance, and that I might turn with all my heart to the Lord my God, who pitieth the youth of my ignorance, and kept me before I knew Him, ..."

Patrick had a personal living faith in Jesus Christ as his Saviour and Lord and he preached the message of the Gospel so that others might turn to the Saviour and find in Him eternal life.

He referred to the people of God as 'His people which He purchased'. Patrick knew that on the cross of Calvary Jesus Christ paid the penalty for our sin. The work of the cross was a work of redemption.

HEAVEN AND HELL

As regards the state of the soul between death and the Judgement Day, Patrick speaks only of hell and paradise. There is no reference in his writings to the Roman Catholic doctrine of purgatory and indeed we should not expect it for this only became official Roman Catholic teaching during the papacy of Gregory the Great who died in 604.

Those doctrines and practices which are distinctive to the Roman Catholic church such as transubstantiation, prayer to the saints or the cult of relics were unknown in the church of Patrick and are not mentioned in his writings. This is only to be expected for they were developed at a later date and were unknown in the apostolic and early post-apostolic church. For example, transubstantiation was not made a Roman Catholic dogma until the year 1215.

THE MYTHS

After his death myths and legends about Patrick began to appear. T O'Raifeartaigh states:

> "Before the end of the 7th century Patrick had become a legendary figure and the legends have continued to grow."
>
> [Encyclopaedia Britannica 13:1077]

Indeed many of the most famous incidents associated with Patrick, such as the use of the shamrock to explain the Trinity to the king at Tara, the lighting of the Paschal fire on the hill of Slane and the destruction of the idol Crom Cruach are later apocryphal accretions with no basis in fact at all.

MYTH No 1   Patrick was sent to Ireland by Pope Celestine I.

Irish political leaders and Roman Catholic churchmen have long associated Patrick and Rome. A former prime minister of the Irish Republic observed in a public address that:

> "The Irish remain steadfast in their devotion to the Faith of Saint Patrick and in their loyalty to the Apostolic See."
>
> [Irish Press 26 June 1961]

But there is no evidence to link Patrick with Rome. Patrick's mission was sanctioned by God, not by Rome. In the *Confession* Patrick tells us how he came to Ireland but nowhere in that document does he make any mention of Rome. In fact, in his writings Patrick NEVER refers to a commission from Rome. That silence is significant. In his *Confession* Patrick defends himself against the charge of having taken too much upon himself in coming to convert the Irish. Surely if the Pope had sent him he would have mentioned that fact in his defence.

At a later date we see Columba also setting out on an evangelistic expedition without seeking a papal commission. This is only to be expected because the ancient church in the British Isles was independent of Rome.

There is **no** contemporary evidence to support the claim that Patrick was sent by the Pope but there is strong and substantial evidence to the contrary, evidence which is too powerful to be set aside.

MYTH No 2   Patrick's mission was endorsed by Pope Leo I.

The Annals of Ulster record under the year 441:
> "Leo ordained 42nd Bishop of the Church of Rome, and Patrick the Bishop was approved in the Catholic faith."

From this Bury deduced that Patrick visited Rome during the time of Pope Leo I.
> "The ordination of Leo is wrongly placed in the Annals in 441; it belongs to 440. But its close association with the notice of St Patrick's *probatio* shows the meaning of the words *probatus est*; and in fact there is no conceivable meaning than formal approval by the Church, and the only form that approval was likely to take in such a case was the approval of the Church's chief representative, the Bishop of Rome."

However, the records of Pope Leo I (440-461) who was Pope during the time of Patrick's ministry contain no reference to Patrick at all.

It was long after the time of Patrick, when Roman influence was beginning to be exerted in the church, that pro-Roman writers became anxious to associate Patrick with Rome and so deny the independence of the early British church. It was for this reason that they began to invent stories about Patrick receiving a commission from Rome or making a pilgrimage to Rome.

MYTH No 3   Patrick was canonised by the Roman Catholic Church.

Patrick was never canonised by Rome and the designation of 'saint' was the outcome of popular tradition. However, he was a saint in the true Biblical sense for he was a true Christian.

MYTH No 4   Patrick wore the ecclesiastical dress of the Roman Catholic Church.

At Saul, on the edge of Slieve Patrick, stands a great stone statue of Patrick, which was erected by the Roman Catholic Church to mark the 1500th anniversary of Patrick's landing in Ulster. The project was initiated on 3 November 1931 and the statue was dedicated by Cardinal MacRory on 12 June 1938. It portrays a bearded Patrick dressed in the robes of a 17th century Roman Catholic bishop, wearing a Roman mitre on his head and carrying a crosier. Yet the mitre was not invented until at least 500 years after Patrick.

This image of Patrick is widespread throughout Ireland. It is found at Tara, Croaghpatrick, Lough Derg and many other places. The statue outside Saint Patrick's Roman Catholic Church in Belfast is another typical example. It is the most common depiction of Patrick but it is an anachronism and it dates only from the early 17th century.

The earliest known example of this genre appeared as the frontispiece to a collection of Irish saints' lives, which was published in Paris in 1624. With that publication a new 'tradition' was born and it has changed little since then. This version of Patrick appeared on the obverse of a copper coin issued in 1798 and this ensured its widespread acceptance.

Even today this remains the preferred image of Patrick in Roman Catholic circles and it serves the purpose for the Roman Catholic Church of claiming Patrick and linking him with Rome.

MYTH No 5   **Patrick used the shamrock to explain the Trinity.**

There is no mention of this in any of the writings of Patrick or in any of the medieval lives of the evangelist. How far back then does this story go?

The first time that the shamrock was associated with Patrick was on coins issued by the Roman Catholic Confederation of Kilkenny in 1645. On one side of the coin was a depiction of Patrick, in the robes, mitre and crosier of a contemporary Roman Catholic bishop, holding out a leaf of shamrock to the people. These coins became known as 'Saint Patrick's money'.

Although the tradition had existed for many years the first written reference to the story is found in a treatise on Irish plants written by the botanist Caleb Threlkeld in 1727. He refers to 'the current tradition that by this three-leafed grass, he [Saint Patrick] emblematically set forth to them the mystery of the Holy Trinity.'

At about the same time that it became associated with Patrick, in the late 17th and early 18th century, the shamrock seems to have acquired its use as an emblem of Ireland. However the story of Patrick and the shamrock is simply a myth created about a thousand years after his death.

MYTH No 6   Patrick drove the snakes of Ireland into the sea.

The first reference to Patrick banishing snakes from Ireland occurs in the writing of Giraldus Cambrensis (Gerald of Wales) who visited Ireland in 1183 and again in 1185. On the second occasion he wrote a report entitled *The History and Topography of Ireland*. In this he mentioned the legend that Saint Patrick banished the snakes and reptiles from Ireland but said that he doubted this 'pleasant conjecture'. Giraldus boasted that he had made no use of earlier commentators or hagiographers and, if that is true, it indicates that the story was an accepted piece of oral tradition by 1185.

There are several versions of this legend but one version tells that he called all the snakes in Ireland together, put them into a box and threw the box into the sea. That is why there are no snakes in Ireland today and the Irish Sea is rough because the snakes are trying to get out of the box!

In some places there are local variations and additions to the story. For example, in the Galtee Mountains, situated between the counties of Cork and Tipperary, there are seven lakes. In one of these, called Lough Dilveen, it is said that Patrick, when banishing the snakes, chained a monster serpent telling him to remain there until Monday!

But the fact is that long before the time of Patrick there were no snakes in Ireland. Even in the 3rd century AD Gaius Julius Solinus wrote:
>"In that land there are no snakes, birds are few, and the people are inhospitable and warlike."

[The Living Legend of St Patrick p 75]

What then is the significance of the story? There are several possible answers.
> **1.** The supposed 'banishment' of the snakes may simply be an invention which was part of the development of a mythology about Patrick, another of the spurious miracles.
> **2.** The story may previously have been attributed to a pre-Christian figure and then later transferred to Patrick.

3. Snakes or serpents were prominent in the old pre-Christian religion of Ireland. The snake represented the underworld, death, healing, renewal and fertility. The banishment of the snakes may relate to the banishment of snake-worship, which occurred as Patrick preached the gospel and men and women turned from the old religion to Christ.

4. The story may be of Norse origin and may be based on a confusion between the Norse word for toad-expeller (Pad-rekr) and the Gaelic form of Patrick (Padraig). This theory is supported by the fact that the association between Patrick and snakes cannot be traced before the establishment of Viking settlements in Ireland.

<u>MYTH No 7</u>   Patrick performed many other marvels and wonders.

Even in the earliest accounts of Patrick many spurious miracles were attributed to him or associated with him Here are some of those recorded by Muirchu:

● Patrick prayed to God to expel Coroticus from this world and from the next. In answer to the prayer and before the eyes of his followers, Coroticus was changed into a fox!

● One of Patrick's young disciples, Benignus, went with him to pray in the middle of a river. Benignus said that the water was too cold and so Patrick sent him to the lower river. There Benignus found the water too hot and had to go out on to dry land.

● Patrick's charioteer was very distressed because he had lost his horses and could not look for them in the dark. Patrick raised his hand and his five fingers lit up like lights. The charioteer was then able to find the horses.

● On the day of Patrick's death there was no night, nor did night fall in Ulster for twelve days after.

But Patrick never claimed that he could perform miracles. His ministry was characterised by hard work rather than spectacular events. He spoke of 'the flock of the Lord increasing in Ireland as a result of hard work.'

APPENDICES

APPENDIX 1
CROSS OF SAINT PATRICK

The origin of the red saltire which is described as the Cross of Saint Patrick has often been explained by reference to the Order of the Knights of Saint Patrick, which was instituted in 1783. It is said that prior to this there was no heraldic symbol associated with Patrick and that the red diagonal cross was borrowed from the arms of the Fitzgerald family and included in the coat of arms of the Order.

However a flag bearing a red saltire was carried by the Catholic Confederates in 1644. Even before that in 1612 a saltire appeared in the arms of Trinity College. But the most significant fact, as regards a connection between the cross and Patrick, is that a saltire was featured on the old seal of the Dean and Chapter of Armagh.

This earlier use of the saltire tends to disprove the Fitzgerald explanation of the origin of the cross.

APPENDIX 2
PATRICK, BRIGID AND COLUMBA

There is a tradition that Patrick, Brigid and Columba are buried together in Downpatrick but the evidence for this is dubious and contradictory.

In the 12th century King Henry II granted the counties of Antrim and Down to the Anglo-Norman knight John de Courcy. He arrived in Ireland in 1177 with a force of 330 men and headed north to Ulster. He captured Downpatrick and within six months he was in control of Ulster. De Courcy established a stronghold in Downpatrick and imposed his authority over the area. According to Giraldus Cambrensis (Gerald of Wales) the remains of Patrick, Brigid and Columba were taken up c1185 and buried in Downpatrick. This was done in the presence of Cardinal Vivian and John de Courcy and was an attempt by de Courcy to placate the local people. John de Courcy also changed the dedication of the cathedral from the Holy and Undivided Trinity to Saint Patrick. The original dedication was restored by King James I in 1609.

46

However the Four Masters give a different account. They relate that in 1293 Nicholas MacMaolisa, having had a revelation that the three saints were buried in Saul, had the bodies disinterred. Great miracles were wrought by the relics and they were finally deposited together in a shrine.

These stories are so contradictory that they may safely be rejected.

APPENDIX 3
LOUGH DERG

The most famous of all pilgrimages in Ireland is that to *Saint Patrick's Purgatory*, which is on a small island in Lough Derg in Donegal. It was believed that a cave on the island was the entrance to purgatory!

Lough Derg is about four miles from the village of Pettigo, which lies on the Donegal - Fermanagh border, and there is a legend that Patrick spent forty days there in fasting and prayer. Later a monastery was established on Lough Derg and it is mentioned as a place of pilgrimage in the *Annals of Ireland* in 784 but the monastery was destroyed by the Vikings about the year 836. The Canons Regular of Saint Augustine took charge of Lough Derg in 1135. They had been sent from Armagh, probably by Malachy.

The medieval legend of Saint Patrick's Purgatory began with the pilgrimage to Lough Derg of a soldier known as the Knight Owen in 1147. The Roman Catholic doctrine of purgatory was still evolving in the 12th century and the story of his visit to the cave known as *Saint Patrick's Purgatory* helped to explain the new doctrine. Over the next 200 years the legend gained general acceptance as it spread across Europe and pilgrims came from many lands to visit the island cave. The 'purgatory' was a cave in which, after fifteen days of fasting and prayer, the pilgrim was locked for a twenty-four hour vigil. During this he was supposed to suffer the horrors of purgatory. The ordeal of the pilgrim was further embellished in the 14th century for, before entering the cave, he had to lie in a coffin while a requiem mass was celebrated! The modern pilgrimage of three days is a rather modest affair in comparison with the medieval one.

In 1497 pilgrimages to Lough Derg were banned by Pope Alexander VI but pilgrims continued to come and the Vatican soon changed its mind.

A few years later in 1503 a Papal Bull cancelled the ban and granted indulgences to all who made the pilgrimage.

Today the pilgrimage season runs from 1 June to 15 August and the numbers going on to the island during that period have fluctuated over the years. At the end of the last century 2,000 to 3,000 arrived each year. After the second World War there was a marked increase with a record 32,000 pilgrims in 1952. There was a falling off in the early 1970s but the visit by the Pope to Ireland in 1979 boosted the numbers for several years. In recent years the average number of pilgrims is around 26,000 a year.

There is an organised three day programme of prayer and penance. The first night is spent without sleep; only on the second night are the pilgrims allowed to sleep in the hostel on the island. Nourishment is confined to bread and black tea made from the water of the lake.

Patrick may have visited Lough Derg but it does not appear in any of the early works about Patrick, not even in Tirechan's detailed list of places which he visited and churches which he founded. Neither does the name appear in the *Tripartite Life*. Lough Derg is not mentioned by Jocelin, although a description of it was added by another writer to some later editions. However Giraldus, writing around the same time as Jocelin (1185), describes "a lake on the bounds of Ulster containing a double island ... called Saint Patrick's purgatory". By then the legend was becoming established.

Peter Harbison suggests that the association with Patrick may have been invented by the Augustinians who came to Lough Derg around 1135.

> "In the absence of a link between the lake and St Patrick dating from before the 12th century, it would not be unjustified to suggest that it was the Augustinians who first popularised St Patrick's connection with the lake, linked him to a Cave on one or other of the major islands, and possibly even created the legend of the Cave in order to increase the pilgrimage traffic."
>
> [Pilgrimage in Ireland p 67]

The Basilica of Saint Patrick on the island was consecrated in May 1931 by Cardinal MacRory, Roman Catholic Archbishop of Armagh, and raised to the status of Minor Basilica by Pope Pius XI.

APPENDIX 4
CROAGH PATRICK

Croagh Patrick (2510 feet) is an isolated and imposing mountain in County Mayo, on the west coast of Ireland.

In Tirechan, there is one brief paragraph about Patrick and the mountain now known as Croagh Patrick but in the *Tripartite Life* this is expanded to four pages. The story claims that Patrick spent forty days and forty nights fasting on the mountain during Lent. Later the legend was embellished even further and it was said that Patrick cast the snakes out of Ireland during his stay at Croagh Patrick.

Croagh Patrick has been described as, "the most climbed mountain in Ireland" but the climbers are Roman Catholic pilgrims rather than mountaineers or hill-walkers. In around 1607 Pope Paul V granted a concession of indulgences to pilgrims to Croagh Patrick.

At the end of the last century Dr McEvilly, Archbishop of Tuam, tried to transfer the centre of pilgrimage to the foot of the mountain but old traditions die hard and in 1903 the modern pilgrimage to Croagh Patrick was revived by his successor Dr Healy, who was responsible for building the present church on the summit.

Originally the annual penitential climb to the summit took place on St Patrick's Day but the weather in March was often too severe and so the pilgrimage was changed to the last Sunday in July, which is known as 'Garland Sunday'. Until the 1970s the climb was made during the hours of darkness but it now takes place in daylight.

The historian John J Dunne describes the pilgrimage to Croagh Patrick in his book *Shrines of Ireland.*

> "Legend has it that it was on this mountain that St Patrick spent the entire Lent of the year 441 in prayer and fasting. In emulation, for countless years, pilgrims have scaled these painful slopes in their bare feet to reach the small plateau, about half an acre in extent, ... Here, on days of pilgrimage, Mass is celebrated continuously in the open air, confessions are heard in the small St Patrick's Chapel and pilgrims follow the Stations of the Cross across the rugged stones."
>
> [Shrines of Ireland p 129]

On the summit of the mountain is the so-called Saint Patrick's Bed, where prayers are said by the pilgrims. In the 19th century this was mainly visited by childless women who slept in the bed at night in the hope of having children.

The name Croagh Patrick links the mountain with Patrick but it was actually a place of pagan pilgrimage in pre-Christian times and the first association with Patrick was long after his death, probably some time around the late 7th century. This was part of the process at that time of developing the cult of Patrick, as seen in Tireachan, and also of absorbing persistent pagan practices into the church.

In her book *The Festival of Lughnasa*, the folklorist Maire MacNeill has pointed to the probability that Croagh Patrick was one of many places in Ireland where the festival of the pagan god Lug was celebrated. According to local tradition the proper day for performing the pilgrimage is *Aoine Chrom Dubh*, the Friday of Crom Dubh, and Crom Dubh was almost certainly a pagan deity.

Another pagan association is seen in the road known as Saint Patrick's Road, which leads to Croagh Patrick from Cruachan, seat of the prehistoric kings of Connaught. According to Peter Harbison:

> "One possible indication of a pre-Christian origin for the road is the presence on it, at Boheh, of a large boulder called St Patrick's Chair, which is decorated with small circular hollows in the stone known as cup-marks, which are generally considered to date from the Bronze Age."

[Pilgrimage in Ireland p 139,140]

APPENDIX 5
STRUELL WELLS

About a mile from Saul are the Struell Wells. For many centuries these four wells were regarded by Roman Catholics as 'holy wells' which were associated with Patrick and which supplied water with special curative powers. A fast-flowing stream runs, partly underground, through the valley and along it are ranged five stone buildings. The site was certainly used in medieval times but the earliest written reference to the Struell Wells was in the 1306 taxation roll and none of the surviving buildings is earlier than about 1600. The earliest accounts of Patrick make no mention of the wells at Struell.

At the site is a stone 'chair of Patrick' which is surrounded by a circular path of sharp stones. Acts of penance were carried out at this site and these involved the penitent crawling on his knees round the circle seven times and then sitting on the chair. Pilgrims also came to bathe in the water in hope of obtaining cures for their ailments. The wells were frequented over many centuries, especially on St John's eve and the Friday before Lammas. However such days became occasions for 'drunkenness and debauchery'. In the 19th century this provoked church opposition and the pilgrimages gradually died away but small groups continued to come until recent times.

Like other 'holy wells', almost all of which are associated with some Christian saint, the tradition of their curative properties predates the Christian era and is of pagan origin. It is significant that the dates of the visits to the Struell Wells, Midsummer Eve and the Friday before Lammas, were festival days in the pre-Christian religion of Ireland.

APPENDIX 6
CROM CRUACH

There is an old story about Patrick overturning the stone circle of Crom Cruach at Mag Slecht, in County Cavan, which is sometimes described as the chief idol of Ireland. But this story is simply another invention. In *The Mountains of Ireland* Dr D C C Pochin Mould writes:

> "Unfortunately for the story this particular stone circle seems to have been a recumbent one from its very building and the Patrician incident an invention to explain the way in which the twelve low boulders were arranged around a taller one which tilted over to the west. There never was a national idol of Crom Cruach or Croich."

[The Mountains of Ireland p 77]

APPENDIX 7
'RELICS' OF SAINT PATRICK

There are three 'relics' which have been closely associated with the name of Patrick.

Saint Patrick's Bell

The Black Bell of Saint Patrick is an iron bell which dates fron the fifth century but there is no real evidence to prove that it was actually used by Patrick. However it was given a splendid shrine around 1100 and was used in the annual pilgrimage to Croagh Patrick. Pilgrims passed the bell three times sunwise around the body, as modern pilgrims do with a stone at Glencolmcille today, and then kissed three times a cross engraved on the bell.

The bell was in the possession of its hereditary keepers, the Geraghty family, until the last traditional steward sold it to Sir William Wilde. Through him it came to its present home in the National Museum in Dublin. However there is not a trace of a cross on the bell in Dublin and so we must assume that either the kissing of the cross wore it away or else Sir William Wilde bought a different bell!

Saint Patrick's bell, was used during the closing ceremonies of the 31st International Eucharistic Congress in Dublin in 1932 and again during the visit of Pope John Paul in 1979.

The Shrine of Saint Patrick's Hand

The traditional Roman Catholic belief regarding this shrine is that it dates back to the end of the twelfth century and was made to contain a bone from the arm of Patrick. When Edward Bruce invaded Ulster in 1316 he removed the shrine and nothing further is heard of it for some centuries, when it is found in the possession of the Magennis family of Iveagh. Later it was handed over to the Roman Catholic priest in Portaferry and eventually came into the custody of the Roman Catholic Bishop of Down and Connor. It was customary for water to be poured through the shrine and then used as a cure for various diseases but when the shrine was opened by Bishop Cornelius Denvir in 1856 it contained no relic at all, only a piece of wood. The shrine is now in the Ulster Museum.

Crosier of Jesus

The *Bachall Iosa* (Crosier of Jesus) was supposed to have been received directly from heaven by Saint Patrick. It was burned by Protestant reformers in Dublin in 1538.

APPENDIX 8
SAINT PATRICK'S BREASTPLATE

The prayer known as *Saint Patrick's Breastplate* or *Saint Patrick's Lorica* first appears in the *Tripartite Life*. The tradition associated with it is that it was written by Patrick and used on the occasion of his supposed visit to the court of King Laoghaire at Tara. However, this 'visit' was a later invention.

Most modern scholars assign the *Breastplate* to the 8th century, long after Patrick. However, as George Otto Simms explains, the *Breastplate* reflects the faith and the theology of Patrick.

> "Many years after his death, the prayers he used were woven into a song called 'St Patrick's Breastplate' (the Lorica). These words echoed Patrick's feelings and experience. They catch the spirit of his newly found faith."
>
> [The Real Story of Patrick p 28,29]

The best-known translation of *Saint Patrick's Breastplate* is that by the Ulster hymnwriter Mrs Cecil Frances Alexander. She made her translation for use on Saint Patrick's Day in 1889 at the request of Rev H H Dickenson, Dean of the Chapel Royal at Dublin Castle.

I bind to myself today
The strong power of an invocation of the Trinity,
The faith of the Trinity in Unity,
The Creator of the Elements.

I bind to myself today,
The power of the Incarnation of Christ, with that of His Baptism,
The power of the Crucifixion, with that of His Burial,
The power of the Resurrection, with the Ascension,
The power of the coming to the Sentence of Judgement.

APPENDIX 9
PATRICK AS A PERSONAL NAME

At present Patrick is one of the most popular names in Ireland but writing in 1834 O'Donovan said:

> "I do not believe that Patrick as the name of a man is a hundred and fifty years in use."

[Gaelic Personal Names p 152]

In the centuries after Patrick's death, the name was not a common name for boys and the first prominent Irishman named Patrick was the military leader Patrick Sarsfield, twelve centuries later. It was the reformation and the plantation which restored the name of Patrick to its rightful place. Patrick came into use as a personal name among the Ulster-Scots and Ulster-English planters before it became common among the Irish themselves.

BIBLIOGRAPHY

Jonathan Bardon: A History of Ulster. Belfast, 1992

J C Beckett: A Short History of Ireland. London, 1952

William Bell & N D Emerson (eds): The Church of Ireland AD 432-1932. Dublin, 1932

G A Chamberlain: St Patrick: His Life and Work. Dublin, 1932

Patrick Corish: The Irish Catholic Experience. Dublin, 1985

E Estyn Evans: Irish Folk Ways. London, 1957

Paul Gallico: The Steadfast Man. London, 1958

R P C Hanson: The Life and Writings of the Historical Saint Patrick. New York, 1983

Peter Harbison: Pilgrimage in Ireland. London, 1991

Alannah Hopkin: The Living Legend of St Patrick. London, 1989

Kathleen Hughes: Early Christian Ireland: Introduction to the Sources

Hugh Kearney: The British Isles.

Donal A Kerr: Saint Patrick. London, 1983

W S Kerr: The Independence of the Celtic Church in Ireland. London, 1931

Harold G Leask: Irish Churches and Monastic Buildings I (The First Phases and the Romanesque). Dundalk, 1955

Henry J Monck Mason: Religion of the Ancient Irish Saints

D D C Pochin Mould: The Mountains of Ireland. Dublin, 1976

Donnchadh O'Corrain & Fidelma Maguire: Gaelic Personal Names. Dublin, 1981

E E O'Donnell: The Annals of Dublin. Dublin, 1987

Liam de Paor (ed): Milestones in Irish History. Cork, 1986

Henry E Patton: History of the Church of Ireland. Dublin, 1907

William Reeves: Ecclesiastical Antiquities of Down, Connor and Dromore. Dublin, 1847

John Ryan: Irish Monasticism. Dublin, 1986

George Otto Simms: The Real Story of Patrick. Dublin, 1993

John R Walsh & Thomas Bradley: A History of the Irish Church. Blackrock, 1991